AF342464

THE ANGER SCALE

THE ANGER SCALE
by Katie Degentesh

Published by Combo Books
Book Design by Christian Palino
Printed in Canada

For subscriptions or to contact Combo Arts, write to:
Michael Magee (Executive Director)
Combo Arts
7 Old West Wrentham Road
Cumberland, RI 02864

or email:
combomagazine@comboarts.org

Grateful acknowledgement is made to the editors of the journals and online publications in which many of these poems first appeared: *The Brooklyn Rail, Coconut, Jacket Magazine, LIT, New American Writing* and *www.personnagesobscurs.com*

Warm thanks as well to *The Anger Scale's* first champions in the Flarflist Collective, where many of these poems received raucous acclaim: Maria Damon, Jordan Davis, Benjamin Friedlander, Nada Gordon, Mitch Highfill, Rodney Koeneke, Michael Magee, Sharon Mesmer, K. Silem Mohammad, Rod Smith, Gary Sullivan and, very especially, Drew Gardner.

TABLE OF CONTENTS

48) SOMETIMES I FEEL AS IF I MUST INJURE EITHER
MYSELF OR SOMEONE ELSE

50) MY TABLE MANNERS ARE NOT QUITE AS GOOD
AT HOME AS WHEN I AM OUT IN COMPANY

52) SOMEONE HAS BEEN TRYING TO POISON ME

54) AS A YOUNGSTER I WAS SUSPENDED FROM
SCHOOL ONE OR MORE TIMES FOR CUTTING UP

56) I AM NOT AFRAID TO HANDLE MONEY

58) I LOVED MY FATHER

60) I LOVED MY MOTHER

62) THE ONLY MIRACLES I KNOW OF ARE SIMPLY
TRICKS THAT PEOPLE PLAY ON ONE ANOTHER

63) I COMMONLY WONDER WHAT HIDDEN REASON
ANOTHER PERSON MAY HAVE FOR DOING
SOMETHING NICE TO ME

64) AT TIMES I HAVE VERY MUCH WANTED TO
LEAVE HOME

66) EVERYTHING IS TURNING OUT JUST LIKE THE
PROPHETS OF THE BIBLE SAID IT WOULD

68) SOMETIMES I AM STRONGLY ATTRACTED BY THE
PERSONAL ARTICLES OF OTHERS SUCH AS SHOES,
GLOVES, ETC. SO THAT I WANT TO HANDLE OR
STEAL THEM THOUGH I HAVE NO USE FOR THEM

69) THERE IS VERY LITTLE LOVE AND
COMPANIONSHIP IN MY FAMILY AS COMPARED
TO OTHER HOMES

71) IT DOES NOT BOTHER ME PARTICULARLY TO SEE
ANIMALS SUFFER

72) MY SLEEP IS FITFUL AND DISTURBED

ABOUT THIS BOOK

I DO NOT TIRE QUICKLY

Even if your heart is messy, I will clean it up.
I have no sense of touch, I do not hear the events around me
and haven't even had a fever for many years.
Since I started using I find I can be much more precise.

I take medicine to fix problems caused by my
burning up energy foolishly as I did when I was trying
to arrange life to suit myself.
As soon as the light comes in, I go to play tennis.

Talking listlessly into my hand,
I am able to inhale much more deeply
to work longer and fill more baskets.
I now go for long walks with my dog

No hurt or fear penetrates my heart.
My elbow is better now too,
and my neck and my numb thumb
belong to disgraced executives of Enron.

They try to turn a wartime walkie
into the beginning of scientific Islamic research.
They get angry, flustered, desperate
and even consumed over other humans.

And even though I haven't won a game yet (!!!)
the breath of life is vivid and arresting.
I like to think in hours instead of days.
When I eat, when I rest from a day's work, later in my bed, and so on.

Bertolt Brecht must not be seen
hoping and un-hoping among so many crickets
armed with slingshots and cap guns,
his secrets kept safe in snow forts.

He is the main reason I watch this schlock.
The muscles in my arms are starting to show.
Then the sun comes out
to admire its shapes —

Each cut is a treasure.
I live among them and they breathe forth fire
and dogma-spewing Dynasty toadies.
I no longer have restless leg.

The unusual still pursues me.
Unfortunately, tennis has become a rarity
Or I would be the first to join the Communist party
When the battles of the mountains are behind us.

NO ONE CARES MUCH WHAT HAPPENS TO YOU

when Serbs get mad, they talk
about a small town like Grace

Stop laughing; I'm serious
Grace is all I can afford on my nursing home wages.

I pity her for the thankless job of building
A nation of Americans conceived in petri dishes.

Whores are disposable.
They get strangled, beaten, tortured, raped …

in old motels, diners, train stations, or whatever,
and I think about Capri Sun bags when it happens.

As he unzips his pants I realize that I'm
what happens to us when the curtain goes down

no one cares much for the body parts
murderer creeping up behind her

Look, poetry, painting, writing …
People don't get it like they should.

But it exists because it's a link to what we can
accomplish through our Academic Plan

no matter how public it all seems
there's a forced casualness to this conversation

I've been out here shooting long enough
I know even a public toilet will net you jail time

because when it comes to that word, "nigger,"
— I know that this is illegal —

it's like the emergence of yet another guilty, white Southern male
as the fat lady continues to sing,

"when they were first created the thing
was to make them as white as possible"

as long as we are laughing
at Rush Limbaugh's addiction

remember that Mt. Rushmore was itself
the creation of an ardent member of the Ku Klux Klan

I SOMETIMES TEASE ANIMALS

because my husband and I have given one another
the freedom to stay alive and growing, we

have never engaged in serious investigation
of the nature of Being in any of the more august

forms of child abuse or verbal harassment
(plus telepathy from the sitter or other living persons)

My son takes showers for the longest time and
he has the cutest bounce to his little step

the backs of his legs look like the little lines on a road map
I'll snip them off and make pillowcases out of them

I know what he's doing, masturbating,
being such a tightwad just makes plain sense

in a world where everyone's someone's private dancer, boy toy
and we will not worry where our water came from

The houses in this town are very neat
The seats are the products of the forest
And are covered with people of both sexes

Whenever we gently stroke a little pet, or give a surprise gift
the wicked boys do sometimes tease the old
by shouting "police, police" on these occasions

and shock the politeness of the inhabitants of the town
– Oh My PetPet! This is Pork, my Zebbra!

When I first start to get to know people
especially some sad seedy tosser

I tell them about my son having this lust
for someone else's small perky breast

and that although I found nursing while walking to be easy
he now buys nothing but wargame manuals

She looked at me and asked if "Dickson" is my son's name
And do we wrestle as a way of showing our fondness for each other

Then my son gave a pint of gin for a squaw
and lived with her as such until his death

MY SOUL SOMETIMES LEAVES MY BODY

When I'm playing any of the Quake games
I have not had sex, etc.
I have been experiencing some darkness in my soul

that makes me spend a considerable amount of time
looking to give Juan Valdez a serious beating.
I remember how I hurt the Turkish saleswoman, Lulu

while running around trying to use the energy cannon
to take pictures of my plants
Despite this I am mostly genuinely bubbly and happy

I do not hardly know anyone except the mosque crowd
but you can always find a redneck station
for passionate kisses with a semi-conscious Gil Gerard

it was sloppy and bloody and all fucked up,
when I try and translate it back into English
it sounds like the Christian notion that we are born

to read stories of free, unhindered UnaBirths
the bright green "beety"-flavoured leaves
handing all financial responsibilities as

Swifty sends out a rare Lotus to collect the weary.
Finding you, my twin soul, has been the best thing for me.
However I am not sure I'd repeat the process next year.

I want my partner to cut the baby's umbilical cord
it sounds like a turkey being choked … it's safe …
and then proceed to suck face disgustingly

Getting to the sea is a challenge
which sometimes leaves me craving vanilla ice
In love, you feel the most alive when grocery shopping

I CERTAINLY FEEL USELESS AT TIMES

At home watching Entertainment Tonight's latest gab-fest
I don't actually know that
I still have a worthwhile contribution to make.

In the end it is pretty damn reprehensible
to be a younger, more vigorous man than myself.

I want space and immortality
and the pull of a certain "southernness"

I am a old, wire-twisting, engineer/inventor type
who always has the picture-perfect desk

Lest you think my vulgarity not apropos, Tim,
women in this society are oppressed

quality women whom I will know for a long time

they were at some point told by somebody
about peacocks and lilies

It was part of an unspoken ritual
that women had come to expect:

Now is the time to tell her how gorgeous she is
giving her peanut butter sandwiches
stuck together with foreign coins

Secretly it pleased her, and she
held her head higher than ever again

feeling a glory in so rolling
that is four times as dear
as any other in North America

A blog isn't all of a person's life, of course
There is a vague, warm, tingly sensation and
the paintings on leather that get hung on a wall

Are women happy? Is there an answer? All the time?

God loved her, so she could
manage to use the bucket to relieve herself
and she drank the water

You can bet I took a lot of "old man" ribbing, though
she said with the bravado of a girl who always gets
all tied up in her prowess as a "male"

Tim was a great sailor and would be proud
Not like a wimpy girl who always gets her partner to save her
with $300 designer cowboy boots

technology should be allowed to evolve
God will put anyone to use who has the real thing
One time back in 1979 he called an emergency meeting

Then came the massacre of fourteen women
You certainly feel invigorated after that kind of day
It blows the cobwebs back to the sci-fi well

I FEEL UNEASY INDOORS

When I'm near someone missing an arm or a leg
I feel weighed down by clothes,
the faithful and celebrities

Already I have been spanked twice by my new stepdad
sometimes gay guys look at me for more than a moment
right outside the door to the boy's department

I cannot understand science.
It just got done raining like hell outside
and now it's darker than hell inside.

A fire flickered always, regardless
White paper. White wool. In the dark …
…That was almost too much for me

The balloon is obviously greater than
whatever is around me that seems to want to scare me
And my long curly hair is all tangled

At this point, it seems to affect only driving,
but what can be done besides driving?

the two military guys, who sleep outside in the snow as usual
seem creepy and messed-up
as if they talk too loud in restaurants
and think all my days have been misspent
I wish they would tell me who she is

To my delight, even outside the Matrix, she is nonsmoking
and takes her anger out on a rock

The wind swollen by ill-temper
without a single bomb falling

the rubbish that people put in their bodies
pierced her eyes like shards of glass

Faced with the heroicity of this girl
I see not only Mars, but its moons

I told her, "I stand outside the gates of the world
which your sex can make a paradise."
"That is well," she replied, "but I feel uneasy."

I BELIEVE I AM BEING PLOTTED AGAINST

This will be a sincere belief
the emperor kept shouting that the letter
describes one of the nurses in the hospital
having special abilities or "powers"

while most of Europe is nervous,
the boy scout is ready and willing once more
he and the most godly bishop
are well correlated with features coming together

although this is the same boy that spelled president wrong on a poster
an inflated area indicates that the biphasic stimulus
fully supports the positions of General Washington
(he actually died by being strangled by a champion wrestler)

or he may learn how to fight
being controlled by alien forces

the odour of old boots, an old fridge's contents
the importance of the continuation of Jihad
a prayer to Jesus Christ our Lord followed by a report
and Ralgex being liberally applied on limbs

the two-way attention distortion test
would be unsuccessful and fruitless

no evidence of a Halloween attack
or a lost utopia, a peaceful little shtetl

the speaker who mumbles, fumbles through papers
by assuming the masked guise of ancestor Zorro
becomes a well-meaning but ineffectual Mexican president
who hated bringing a new religion to the people

It moves, it gets agitated, it shakes.
Perhaps people are at the seaside and
both Jedi find themselves in mortal danger
The families of Europe were having a tizwaz.

I feel as if I am being plotted against
and the only real way out of it for me
would be pregnancy,
and that may not even save me.

If the average person knew of the evil,
they would pick up pans, ball bats, or anything they could find and
continue to hover uneasily in the "elevated range"

accused of misogyny
by The Greyish Wyrm!

WHEN I AM WITH PEOPLE I AM BOTHERED BY HEARING VERY QUEER THINGS

I went to the pillar-box
I never saw a worse-looking house
in town or in hunting zones

"welcome to girly hell"
turn her out because her necklace has been stolen
explain it by some kind of hypnotism

they fancied those constellations were
able to handle large fires
with the elaborate finish of jewellery

wherever we find pleasure, there we are attached
because of certain "spiritual rappings" or "knockings"
lucky for us that we so rarely knock up against them!

we shall agree at the outset that
The Teacher was just going to
be all things to all men,
to burst in upon them with such excitement
Dwarves started arriving, yes, Dwarves!

Even usually rational people are starting to suspect
the lining of your stomach
his eyes and their fluttering lids

he didn't ride the roan mare he'd been riding
he does not think it will ever be required

please under no circumstances speak of this
smoke your luncheon instead

the lady seems decidedly eccentric
Uncle Roy's Queer Girls
embodied this principle
on screen, in a lesbian way,

A strange creature,
Let us lead him to the elders.

AT TIMES I HAVE FITS OF LAUGHING AND CRYING
THAT I CANNOT CONTROL

Susan picked up a 19-year-old at the reception
and encouraged everyone she knew to do the same

laid on his shoulder and bore him twenty or thirty children
with a wild, staring expression and strabismus of the right eye

The doctor said that was usual.
We were daily overtaken back then
With the mass of hair she had

We had to wait until she left the room
to speak to God about the vibrator,
masturbation and women's sexuality
and the vulgarity of walking

Part of a Sunday my brother and I then used to spend
in walking in the meadows and singing psalms
alternating with intervals of stupidity

But one day, just as we were beginning to sing,
I noticed on the other side of the bath
a rather large circle, set below the hallway proper

she of the hair took the fiery torch
and knelt down with the circle ever growing smaller,
until she was at the center of a group hug
in which she was heartily joined by all the merry party!

then she falls and rolls off the roof onto the ground
into a circle drawn on the floor of the garage
which doubled as a brothel containing two whores
swaying their bodies until by and by their heads were rotating in a large circle

many nasty falls I've taken into the future
are to be ascribed to Susan

OFTEN I FEEL AS IF THERE WERE A TIGHT BAND ABOUT MY HEAD

I have always had a canine spirit with me
Struggling writing out long division for math
With a deep soulful voice

I must bore him to death
On another planet
Playing the Holiday Inn lounge

A gentle, soft young man
Much like a gentle wind or a butterfly

Long-term fungal infection
Tingling down his arm
With his melted taffy voice

A rushed feeling about it
And a young feeling, too, I agree

Thrilling chases and clearly-drawn characters
Agricultural economists and cowboys

Everyone else is a bunch of kooks that surf
I see them around the world on TV

The hobbit hole gives me a real high
With the central bank in the background

The Bible is as dry as dust
With antiseptic and sterile towels draped around it

I SEE THINGS OR ANIMALS OR PEOPLE AROUND ME
THAT OTHERS DO NOT SEE

I am a ghost maniac boy who doesn't like work.
I am an animal with a halo.

My cat comes to visit regularly and I'm so very content
when it thinks I'm going to hit it with a rock!

I see animals and me standing up for peace
Listening to whales sing

I pretend I have a German Shepherd.
A black dog, head held high, standing under a tree.

When the dog owners have a conversation about the dog
I see the ghost of Monty Python

And I can't tell what is serious and what isn't.
Is it supposed to be funny? It is incoherent.

Animals are feeding on their little ones
These animals are not simply annoyed,
as the seal was by the seawater

Cows are incredibly placid, sedentary animals when on the ice
but really they are gay nymphomaniacs
so big and bright that I will need to carve them
a juicy new watermelon.

They also dig pretend burrows
when a human doesn't listen to what they are saying.

The fact remains that no cow has ever been proven to be a ghost or spirit.

Things are good, good is sweet, sweet is gnarly, and gnarly has
the musty reek that reminds me of the cow fetuses
I had to dissect a couple of months ago

It turns out, your cow is actually headless
He possesses supernatural powers
and runs a home-based,
ghost-delivery business

that sells revolution, the immigrant experience,
slavery, westward expansion, tall tales
a swarm of bees and used airmail stamps

Have you ever been guilty of pre-judging someone –
say, an expert in blood-splatter patterns –
then found out that she was dating you only to "save your soul"???

All around me, lesbians were buying houses and having children together
but finally I calmed down by painting a painting
it was basically about Bill Murray and some cow

who looked at the photos and determined that
a man being tortured with Botox and his fat being shot
out of a syringe tip bottle (actually an enema bottle) for three weeks
did not constitute intra-species recycling

because there was more than one species involved.
Cows are not 98% human; they are not even half human.

They are harmless, they look nice, they don't need a box to crap in.
Forty cows accelerate obediently, heading west across the plain.

I HAVE HAD VERY PECULIAR AND
STRANGE EXPERIENCES

And you walk alone, infinitely alone.
And you carry with yourself a flower.
They are made with flour and salt
and they are baked in
the people who stay at night in this valley.

The term, "the seed of the woman,"
was birthed out of a hunger for God.
It began its life as a wrapper for sugar cubes,
white cows moving towards the retina
which have their origin in Christ himself.

Some of these losses were due to some
displacement of the fragment into
a twisted anecdote of lost love
or other gift (sweet, salt, fluid or a flower)

the iris distributes light
because some men required
things that were interesting to play with

galaxies that are contained in larger groups
may take plenty of getting used to
They are wonderfully buoyant

eastern and western famous people
seem to have a fixation for young boys
The whip is an enlargement of the body
and no microscope will make it possible to eavesdrop on it in its sphere of activity

Negroes are human beings
given a considerable position in the political life of Northern Ireland
and all wore moccasins
so as to avoid a misunderstood creativity

Say good morning bossy
You are invited to suffer war, pestilence,
droughts, internal strife, inflation
accompanied by some adjective which explains
things that you would not do in health

If you saw *Blade Runner*, then you had a glimpse
Of the life of every man of God
The day-to-day variation of teeth
But you still probably wouldn't get to do all the things you wish you could.

MY JUDGMENT IS BETTER THAN IT EVER WAS

setting off a fire extinguisher into the crowd
with the villagers of the town
as though you were scattering them to the winds

the piano starting its awesome motif
as Mary and Kitty entered the room
through a sewerage tunnel

Kitty's focus was fixed on the town square,
where she saw her airship
returning to childhood

she told a group of students
anyone that would leave Satan in power
was just a freshman

the risks were not appreciated
because of the wisdom and the power and …
She reached for her handkerchief to wipe them away

Kitty: You smell like it, that's all …
This morning passed as usual

overwhelmed by such a consciousness of depravity
Kitty made a great show of warring with Mary

"How could they fire you and keep tinkerbell," she asked
In what ways has your life changed since you left Mormonism

it's a big old ego bash to find out
on the side of a hill covered with sand interspersed with bushes

that personal bitterness is poor
and the other persons didn't have
half the emotions you had

and very severe was my mental suffering
but management has to go ahead

and Satan is given his kingdom back
his face and bosom covered with thick blood

"My way is permanent," he said
"a very important business judgment"

It was curious how the women clasped their hands,
and lifted them up as if in the extacy of devotion

the people at the ballot-box
in the usual way about missionary things
enjoying a cheering sense of God's love

THERE SEEMS TO BE A LUMP IN MY THROAT MUCH OF THE TIME

About a month ago,
Uncle gave me a lump of gallium to play with

the doctors told me it was nothing to worry about
then the whispering began

one neighbor remembers seeing a woman with an olive
dipping a slice of potato in salt water
to save someone from war

On darts nights thick bread was cut into quarters
and the camera was given hypnotherapy
to remember the old times of the Indian wars

there was a whole lot going on, and a lot of dancing
more rhetoric than committed action

The guard was friendly and soon produced ice
He was just a lump of meat, and he said,
"better than being struck by lightning,
but I just had a baby"

Kick that hat-box under the seat
There seems to be no historical explanation for its presence
except as a perverse celebration of selfishness

no amount of perfume or frilly lace is going to make
a "what's your holy grail" thread
out of tortoise excrement skimming a grave

I'm not a lump of horrified jelly,
but parts of me are scared:

the anvil in my heart
my animal crackers, and another veggie burger
How can I reduce the appearance of them?

Suppose someone on a sailboat photographs a whale
climbing out of the Mediterranean
just as seven-year-old Randy saw his uncle
impale Theresa on the statue.

There seems to be so little one can do about it
over the next few minutes

I AM EASILY DOWNED IN AN ARGUMENT

When the muezzin began the midday call to prayer
Marylyn Putrinski was already in the shower
for a rare eye cancer, her thin voice
weak and trembling in the cascade.

She got into a argument with the lady
who wore a Rainbow around her neck
about Jesus and Satan
and who was better on his computer.

This woman is a perfect fit in a party
she first found Hendrix unconscious
when he knew how to use drugs
and was too intelligent to accidentally overdose

the raging need she felt
with her husband came back to her mind
the tenderest feelings of the parental heart
that were ever reared in Southern slavery

"Mom, where did the beds come from?"
Nature must not win the game, but she cannot lose
with the assistance of her bike bell
she's already "I go back to your place …"

you understand sexual agency,
the softer crackling version that
is exquisitely sweet, and very low
a token, marginal drop in the bucket

a steadily marginalized beverage
like the cold damp spot of her own drool
It was so apparent
that I openly volunteered to play Rocky anytime she does Janet

CRITICISM OR SCOLDING HURTS ME TERRIBLY

Where most other puppies are robust and rowdy
he and his ex are good friends again.

They also dance and they
don't like to talk about it with me.

This is the only problem we have, but
it hurts Chelsea, it hurts the President,
and to see you go through something like this

to reduce my living out the Gospel of Christ
to drinking loads of prune juice to keep the bowels moving

I have to make it with supreme care
to maybe at last find peacefulness.

The sun is an annoyance.
I want someone to grow old with
calling me "Lard Bottom"
to reveal one last glimpse into his soul.

If I could ever bear to stay in the same room as you
in the wake of a hedge-cutting tractor
I'd just … eat, exercise, and not drink any wine,

and the kid grows in me and then
the heir in spirit to the
Bushido Blade swordsmanship simulators

is a managed care executive proud of his record of service
who has my virginity and my only child
but from a friendship standpoint.

Having written such a beautiful story,
You are suddenly a completely different person,
and generally a very terrified person.

I feel there is no other alternative than to
pretend to despise you, yet long for your touch
This is what cold meat has come to represent with many people.

I BELIEVE I AM NO MORE NERVOUS THAN MOST OTHERS

All the friends and family
stop second-guessing what
has killed her clitoris and G-spot.
They need to survive and leave offspring

hunting down friends who are 21
and taking pictures after the ceremony
would result in producing the most attractive
sweater acrobatics

you sense quite clearly whether something has worked or not
the moment, the battle at hand
the death of the clitoris and
the sweet taste of freedom
in the pit of your stomach

The pressures and lines of earth will be gone forever
the sinful body, the seat of sensual lust becomes a corpse
The box on the top shelf.
It was such a great gift.

Childhood mysteries have succumbed
to the incandescent, moonstruck stage
the door to the floor opens

You do about five complete cycles,
back and forth from the pasture like a good girl

Over-masturbating since a young age
the new grips made it easier
the onus on the pre-newbie
"Now that this has happened
we're ready for anything rational,

this is great exercise."
One two three four five, one two three four five.
"You'll know the results instantly."

If it can happen,
I'm no more nervous than I am about living in this city.
I lived through it effortlessly

those with hearts reacted badly
and are a reminder of the type of danger that is in our society
because it is they who are nervous being around me

as my mind wonders to wondrous places
It hurts too much!
"It is when you least expect it they will strike."

The Baron, who had been glowing,
led me into the dim silent library
said his family is planning a trip to Disney World

I chose a lovely pale lavender one and it was
the corporate cockroaches from planet widdley
who weathered the stress without problems

Yet the robin has many good qualities:
he is robust, confident, a straightforward personality,
and no more nervous, perhaps, than many another American.

Bird came to know the private Madonna:
the woman who would sing snatches
and wetness of the inside of her pussy

stuffing the holes of her acoustics and semi-hollows
with illness and medical care items
I wish it was that simple.

It worked! My bike was set free!
The car has a more confident feel to it.
Other side benefits include: new hair growth
No more lying nuns, no more negotiations, no more.

Heart breakdowns with dilated pupils
will infringe upon me today
somewhat prettily and no doubt sweetly

I VERY MUCH LIKE HUNTING

The camera control is simple but
there is a certain level of "twitch factor"
which is in fact welcoming AND
trivial most of the time.

the vision of being a "free agent"
for use in light polluted cities
with a man who trod on my dress
in different overseas countries

Wonderful shot john
Oh, menstrual products have also been inside my vagina
Its mapping and snapping tools are something no-one should miss
I think it got my daughter a better grade in the past semester.

Since it has spread itself into many homes
one may wonder that Johann Sebastian Bach does not appear
looking light and bright and young again
talking about mathematics and lyrics

in the centre of an elegant if fading spa town
to nicely touch women, cuddle, stroke arms, face, hands,
give back and neck massages and lots of warm but non-sexual touch

now and then for fun
and sorry for eating so many
and please keep it that way for future guests
almost gem-like in its small beauty

So I didn't notice when, but
I was falling in love with algae and now

I had spurred myself too quickly to the end.
This is a very interesting game.

They grab what you've got.
Slippery smooth & fun to play.
I wish you of creative good luck.
Just make sure to bring nice shoes.

LIFE IS A STRAIN FOR ME MUCH OF THE TIME

This planet has – or rather had – a problem
it simply feels flat most of the time
the way a few very rich people do now

they leave off the breathing Americans
in solitary confinement
in the arctic winter, when the sky
has a lot of energy
and the mosquitoes are not in full force
(think pill bugs of the sea
involved in bloody feudal wars)

Some were shoddier than others
Some were taught to play on the violin
Some were nobles who had upset the king
Some were actively connected to the actual events

an old lantern lit the men's faces
the mud was at least ankle deep

It was the constant darkness more than the cold
the standard average-student mold

Just as your heart goes out to the man
when you learn that he was abusive and miserable,
sometimes it seems odd that topless bathing isn't allowed

when we give away use of roads
we get too much cheese

five of the six dioramas show
you can trust the federal government
to be cheaper than coal

even the smart kids
burned the good food in front of us
in favor of the articulation of existing paradigms
It is cleaner when burned.

The naive reader may believe that you feel uncomfortable
because of the appearance of your eye and eyelid
But the real problem is that
alcohol was the primary agent for the development of Western civilization
around a large quantity of dog poop

MY HANDS HAVE NOT BECOME CLUMSY OR AWKWARD

Sometimes I find that my hands have become aware of each other,
or that they have become so weak that singing has become impossible.

In addition to the Truth, the pointy spikes on my new car also hurt.
I know that the Principles have sharpened my chops.
I now have the ability to move the bone leading to my right ring finger
back and forth all by itself.

In my cutting tank I have several babies
that can never be washed clean,
icy and shaky and pale-purple
riddled with pomphylix
like Binkie my budgie.

My "Fucnoids" hurt like a mofo
more sensitive as I reach my later 30's
like an old grape with all of the water sucked out

gentle fists resting within my vest pockets
unusually several and arranging them in a thick album
Oh, how I want to make someone happy.

I feel sort of mechanical.
I guess I need some new dish soap.

I used to think that my hands had become mothers
because I looked at my tits every day

Later, I noticed that my piano needs tuning
and was spattered with forty years of pain

place the bridal netting around the plug
and secure it with a rubber band
and in a week it is firmly attached

In the picture below you see my captive raised calm.
These tiny gloves will kill your calm if you do not remove them.

Hi my hands have become suntanned,
Can u please tell me what should I do
I have worked closely with the Militia
To bring back my original color.

I am able to use an intuitive gift to finely tune into your body language
But my hands have become literally black
Pls do give me a good advice to regain my color.
They'll treat me differently. They'll invite me into their homes.

My hands used to be fine, and white, and my friends would take pleasure
scrub and wash and stroke and pat that knead the breasts
that push and roll to get the milk flowing
for a very awkward change into

the shapeless feet of the rhinoceros.
I like the sound of her dry skin
I am also at work on one like one of those meadows I sent you recently.

O my soul, I have given thee everything,
But I note that my hands do not warm back up inside you.

SOMETIMES I FEEL AS IF I MUST INJURE EITHER MYSELF OR SOMEONE ELSE

We are nearing the time when Christ is come
to make recordings for the blind and dyslexic
in Hawaii, and sees nothing but very plain prose.
The dear devoted little fellow! He worshipped that kitten.

When I hear the bugle-horns
I feel as if I am running out of time to confess
those ill chosen and unfortunate words which I spoke last night:
"Oh, Jackal!" "Yes," said the little Jackal.

I am very close with one of the girls I work with
the birds are just shouting outside and everything
seems just shouting for joy — even the trees and things we can't really hear
but I haven't the slightest idea how to reinforce that

I have about as much vitality left as wet blotting paper
the largest fish is sorting pebbles, shoving at them with
doors, windows, cars, traffic lights, bridges, etc.,
anything his precious webbing
would stick to in this rain.

I should like to go back to the pictures once more.
I do not know if I have the ability to enter into mediumship
I have had a few experiences of the Holy Spirit taking over
then again … it could just be cancer hahahahahaha.

At the end of each strip there is tied a sharp piece of bone or stone
Unfortunately for my arteries,
*N Sync's monumental "No Strings Attached"
brings me closer to the end with each stone I move

I must kiss myself ******commenced blowing kisses
vigorously at the gay figure reflected in the glass*******
Yes, that's the same woman.
this was a particularly overzealous breed

After carefully perusing your journal
I must apologize for the birdies
Yes, indeed, this dude started out with a bang.
Go out and purchase this fine, fine text

when these feelings of weakness occur
there is far more of me than I am happy with
I'm not comfortable for some reason.
This is not where I expected to come.

Let me be perfectly honest though, although it might mar the point,
Her left leg is now stretched high in the air to her left.

Willy looks too sweet —
The hand over the vagina …
give yourself up to it with a violence
which I confess I am not able to emulate
Stand and follow the spelling bee format.

I had no idea you were this religious
I must smash my head into the wall.

I prefer writing about on-base percentages, fielding percentages,
and players' performances, but sometimes
I just wish God would give me answers on issues of life.
Then I feel as if I must void my bladder — but instead,
this great outpouring of juices happens.

MY TABLE MANNERS ARE NOT QUITE AS GOOD
AT HOME AS WHEN I AM OUT IN COMPANY

do not cram your hands
down in your pockets
and especially before ladies
by squeezing their thighs
while climbing a rope
in broad daylight without a blush
to take beaver on Salt River

on an extended preaching tour
through the peri-cellular spaces
to seek three stolen princesses

gather some skunk-cabbage
with cool slogans
but do not abandon your boat to do so

Share your arena
with a quiet horse and
the extreme northern part of France
with the brother of the Twistedhair

certain rites of passage into adulthood
are very bad amongst the sheep

I have so many children
and cannot fix them like other children

But the road does not lead to slaughter
because I can not afford it

despite the entreaties and importunities
the shoes would do significant damage

circling a herd along with the Christian pilgrims
with clean white apron and sleeves to match

never thinking to retain them as a private treasure
save one dispatch
of five words

SOMEONE HAS BEEN TRYING TO POISON ME

I have two kids still alive on the 23rd of March 2004
"Here, have another one," said summer, thrusting
the tiny tin of speed at me

actually, it wasn't speed
it was the awakening of nature

bread that smells this good
understands my attitude instantly

That insufferable woman
runs in distressed circles
oozing references to
pizza in Chicago

As I know crowns and wars
the stove is smoking!

apples contained razorblades
and wouldn't go to restaurants

Come hither purposely
with typhus vapours
And I will spit in
the piano room

I'd offer to fuck him
when the soaps are on TV

Assume any shape you like
unless you show me the way
to the ship's rail.

This lamb is telling me that
me, my wife, son and pet
have never discussed this issue

swedish-art-glass me with aloes
or kill me on the stage at night

by gorging yourself on the pits
of microscopic uranium crystals

I got ants in my sugar, baby
and the orange-orchard
is very fond of me

The fourth new tree shouldn't be here
Just when you think you've got
enough, enough grows

My Guinea pig just died
The agony, the scratching, the embarrassment
second-hand nastiness
I want my chlorine gas

A pair of hostile geese
With horseradish
burst into my quarters
I am still well and strong

AS A YOUNGSTER I WAS SUSPENDED FROM SCHOOL
ONE OR MORE TIMES FOR CUTTING UP

Everyone knows about Dallas
and its acts of terrifying gorgeousness

a chef in a tall hat piping meringue
discussing the "brain drain"

dropped a slab of concrete on his left foot
before being lured to the guitar

doesn't recall details of cutting up friend
to create fake masterpiece

when Dorrington came home unexpectedly and found
flight attendants ready to undergo radical surgery

I've been cutting up Vipers more and longer than anyone I know
the severed sea bream head washed down the river on a chopping board

The class batted it around in a bloodless little battle of the sexes
and I just started branching out to dogs and cats.

The boar is cut up and the hounds are fleshed.
So far we've concentrated on the whole hog
a popular euphemism for saying that someone doesn't like
our size and age differences

Like cutting up and depositing the body of a camel
in the drawing of a dinosaur head
and sewing it to other stuff like duck or squab
or radioactively contaminated tools and equipment

I sat on the back of our sofa listening eagerly
constantly at my dad's side fishing
going to the local coin shop with my dad
in small-bore slow-fire events

paths only modern-day Cowboys or Indians would travel

Slice off both sides close to the seed to create two halves of
The Moon, which rises while the men are cutting up the whale carcass.

I AM NOT AFRAID TO HANDLE MONEY

It started with being attacked by a large male pigeon
in a big square in Copenhagen
This was followed by having a boy throw a live chicken at me

a black bird and then a sparrow flew in
through my bedroom window
to loot my life clean

The sun heats up due to fear.
She cannot understand what death is.
She does not think of death, because she does not want to die.

I just refuse to tell her not to do what she does so well.
I also don't like feathers.
Flying is a real pain as in my heart
being inside a pressurized container

My father was attacked by a rooster when he was a kid.
We were visiting a rainforest
where there was one glass tank with one rooster in it.
"stand still and it won't sting you"

I wanted to show him that I did not mind spending money
on you and your juju that cannot see, walk or move
but being in a position of not having money paralyses me.

The worst birds for me are pigeons, sea gulls, swallows and chickens.
I know my fear comes from my father.
The only bird I am not afraid of is the duck and the hummingbird.

I once ran across the road to escape those stripy little flies of evil
like WASPs but it's not really a phobia just fear
I received very little sympathy from my family

Losing my baby to death or anything is practically a fantasy
How evil must a woman be to feel the same contempt for baby birds?

I remember wondering how I would take care of everyone if I am not physical
Already in mourning for my life and for the life
Of giant smiling rats and 7 ft yellow birds

At the seaside there are not so many birds in your face
as there are when the ocean of human beings gets together

I LOVED MY FATHER

I loved my father and I loved Jesus.
What was I to do?
I felt like a canoe
that was being pulled apart by two strong men.

I expressed that eloquently by imitating his life,
by becoming more and more ineffectual daily.

People would generally hide from him
because he looked so American

I didn't know that my father was controlling and manipulative.
I wanted to glorify Him by paying off the debt of sinful man

At least he could've explained why
he didn't want me to play with the toy gun.

He really cared about us.
Maybe he had no feelings towards or against other people, either.

Rather than be exposed to one more sales pitch
They spit on me and I ran away

Nothing happened for almost a year then
He'd call the State Police just to try and settle me down

If you got your finger cut off
on the thought of killing him
He got angry and he wanted to get even.

I love plants and trees, but
I wasn't allowed to go out or talk.

He was a wonderful man,
dealt with the servants of the castle
made a good living and provided well for his family
shared his affections with his boyfriend on weekends

I loved him from afar.
I sucked my thumb until I was six years old.
I didn't realize it at the time.

"When I was your age," he said,
"I had a square piece of white cloth to be made into
firstborn children of God, truly made perfect as God."

He looked at me, and he knew I had stolen it.
A man will be hated by his own family.

I hated Listerine and I hated my father.
I do not know whether he is alive or not.

I took what I wanted, and left him spoiled behind me.
I was reborn in Ireland, in 1753.

I LOVED MY MOTHER

I wished I could run away with my brothers and sisters
but maybe it was more a desire to have her be both dead and alive
in the freezing skies of the north
well wrapped up in a large warm white shawl

while the aspirant would remain perfectly passive
until he or she merged with the Infinite
but my sister really should do something about the way she looks

I loved my mother, and she did nothing
as my father repeatedly beat me.

She was always selfless towards me
even when very sick.

I was the oldest one, except the one that died
she was always scared I'd disappear.

she must have had good qualities
because she helped me believe I could do anything and everything
except for my dreams, the extensions of her soul

She said, "Wayne"
in a voice that conveyed her shame

that caused him to bury himself deeper,
pushing her against (PASSIVE AGGRESSIVE) the miner's prick

She died of old age full of years
and esteemed by all her children

They were nothing like those limp squares
she was always concerned about

She was always very smart even as a puppy.
I really loved my mother as much as a hair can love.

The seeker was in fear, but she was always in fear
so it was only one more thing to frighten her.

I hated my mother for hating cats
but I wanted her to live, and I knew that

in this era of navel gazing,
it was my navel she was always gazing at.

After mastering the rules of grammar
she was like a ghost to all my friends

No one felt they had the right to have her committed
while baking cookies

THE ONLY MIRACLES I KNOW OF ARE SIMPLY TRICKS
THAT PEOPLE PLAY ON ONE ANOTHER

I know God can provide us
with more than one cover story
on the subject of black holes

it's how life was originally created
in the hospital those weeks
after I was electrocuted some 35 years ago
when my mom and I emoted as we'd never had

mustering energy for the "unconscious"
pain and frustrations that we were feeling

I never discussed this with the doctor, but
the seas don't part and mountains
made it really difficult for the whole province
to see pictures of the inside of my uterus

I do know that rule number one
is never to point your camera at the sun.

Just stay home and be a mom!!!
my last boyfriend punched me out
in front of my 5-year-old
and I have never been happier

a woman who learned to bend spoons from Uri Gellar
said that my uterus performed
the function of a small blanket placed over a cat
before giving the cat away or putting her to sleep

Baby dust to all, Sherry

I COMMONLY WONDER WHAT HIDDEN REASON ANOTHER PERSON MAY HAVE FOR DOING SOMETHING NICE TO ME

You should come out betting, unless you think
you have Tourette's, in which case

the real substance of the mosquito,
or of being a mosquito, is alive but hidden
as part of a counterplot through history.

To illustrate, a practicing Catholic would speak of
a faith based on their experience of owning a car —
this is sometimes coolness, and sometimes baditude.

Dick can have several meanings,
so the reason one person is called Dick
is not necessarily the same reason another person is named Dick.

I try to give them a series of little red warning lights:
Ottoman-based secret societies
cut into a round scallop shape

but pigs and little boys sustain
large numbers of small ruptures

When atrocious examples of evil come to Dick's attention,
he again speaks of hidden seeds that God placed in each living thing
this widespread dabbling in the world

hitting the already wounded areas of his body
to brutally murder the alpha asshole of their white trash clique
The world waited and all they saw was the Pope die

People commonly wonder why
he had a hubcap in his house

Was it for global domination?
It actually was his spaceship.

AT TIMES I HAVE VERY MUCH WANTED TO LEAVE HOME

When the time came for Jesus and the apostles to eat, he said,

"Since I began yoga with Michele,
I have very much wanted
to write about this whole thing,
to help my recovery from this,
but I have deliberately refrained from doing so
out of respect for the multiple video game options."

"I have very much wanted
to feel what sex is all about from an early age.
I know that you do not understand,
but I wanted to tell you about
the long festering wound of sadness
that I buried in my uterus for so many years."

"You know I have lain with women in order
to eat this Passover meal with you before I suffer.
It's an exhibit that will be easily accessible to the public."

"I will then be free to join in on one of these trivia nights,
spend quality time mano en mano with the land
in both Indonesia and Australia."

Would He have trusted Western medicine?
He is not listed as a survivor
in the books I have on the Titanic

As far as body piercing goes,
His boys back home catching crocodiles
helped the holy child get
through a painful process

bringing ice to housebound patients (and their carers)
Chien-Chen River is our neighborhood
Contemporary girlswerealsomorelikelytoendorse

My favorite movie has always been the sound of music
We imagine you must deeply miss the shaft

EVERYTHING IS TURNING OUT JUST LIKE THE PROPHETS OF THE BIBLE SAID IT WOULD

Since I just got a haircut today
everything is turning jiggy around me

turning into a sequel or prequel
in anticipation of the colder weather

flowers are blooming, gardens growing
water flowing, the wildlife is there

but the housing is too expensive
for you to retain your status bar

when it flashes red you're getting hurt
Yeah! You're a star fucker, star fucker, star fucker,

so addicted to Wayne Gilchrest, the superhero, that
the heavens have refused to yield their accustomed amount of rain

While at the gym getting sweaty
The grumbling turns into a sustained roar

there has been and is now considerable sickness
but it turned out to be just a cosmic accident

the yellow giants are up
against a number of Yemeni lawyers

where they can talk with the pennies
more like heated brass than anything else

a simple rewording, such as changing "man" to "pennies"
and I don't feel stressed anymore

Batman is still at home in a sick furl
stuck between miscarriage and tubal pregnancy

I'd leave a message on his answering machine
But I want to come back here and read only happy things

I wouldn't believe the bible if it said the sky was blue
Just go to Vegas and do the things you wanna do

SOMETIMES I AM STRONGLY ATTRACTED BY THE PERSONAL ARTICLES OF OTHERS SUCH AS SHOES, GLOVES, ETC. SO THAT I WANT TO HANDLE OR STEAL THEM THOUGH I HAVE NO USE FOR THEM

Taking on an avant-garde artistic attitude
that gives selfish personal power
he threw himself into the adventure of his first abstract
But no leader lives forever

he had a successful first year, at the end of which
he went to Athens in order
to become a member of
the impersonal features of the Lord

his "Hermit Songs"
were "written by monks …
with the desire to support a gay-owned business
and a one-on-one relationship"

his loveableness and sincerity
had been driven by female consumers
who were attracted
by the personal atmosphere
of thin-skinned people

and the national reputations of the chemistry
between herself and her young kinsman
the choice benefits of spiritual maturity
the personal magnetism of the prophet,
along with the power of his or her message

doing these difficult jobs well
under the influence of Alcibiades
beyond holding them in a file
Here corporate sponsorship is
approaching the Absolute Truth

THERE IS VERY LITTLE LOVE AND COMPANIONSHIP IN MY FAMILY AS COMPARED TO OTHER HOMES

With everyone doing their own thing
all he does is stand on his head and win games
while trying to suck blood out of a turnip.

He thinks the world today is upside-down;
What counts is waiting on walls
for the arrogant time-pleaser
with his assurances of love braced with sentences.

He is an out-and-out egotist.
He likes his love different to anyone else
But all he wanted to know about was love.

This produces a slave who is also extravagant
He planned to save to produce distinctive,
lifestyle-centered cars for young buyers
but he did not have the spirit of Christ

Who was he? Why wasn't he on the earth?

Because she more than likely came from a home where
here and there the suggestion of an uncomforting pleasure
was shown in such a bountiful way right through the ages

She asked her audience to send in
single-paragraph romance stories.
The stories are amazing … depressing.
In general they mean very little.

She was a big woman, with lots of hair
She felt that her life was being made up
From a book of love stories told by God

Where people are reading
"THE MESSAGE OF THE STARS"
but not jumping into bed with one another.

So much care and effort was put into the dragon
There was very little left on how to perform oral sex.

I saw right away that what these children need
Were books full of lust, sex and deceit
in a way that has previously seemed repulsive to me

where some gimp you'll never hear of again
hugged the woman's knees tightly and prepared
to make the rupture only the more violent

anyone else noticed that this is actually all about people rowing, fighting
even raping one another?

This is an epic which has got nothing heroic about it.
The movie is very slow so do not expect a wild ride.

I mean no offense to those who lost their lives
I don't mean in Germany, either, under the Nazis

I mean people who care passionately for poetry

IT DOES NOT BOTHER ME PARTICULARLY
TO SEE ANIMALS SUFFER

I caught Mrs. Senator looking at the birds
she seemed like just another rich man's wife

a grotesque amalgamation of various species of
grates, dead animals, and fallen tree branches

about to be run over by another "bubba" or "good ol' boy"
particularly if she keeps gobbling on the ground

how does insulting people fix anything?
especially basset hounds

So they saw homosexual behaviors amongst animals.
At least working animals get to rest
to share their success of healing themselves

please forgive me for teaching my plants
are able to change their shape
much more readily than animals

I can also understand people being tetchy and irritable
when they feel provoked by nuisance
or hear the "thump" as they hit them

Splat! Splat! Splat! A part-time vegetarian
hiding during the day in dark
in a cool indoor penguin tank

it beats the heck out of cards
moving the other direction on the rarity chain
particularly when I'm in the shower, or tired

I think that animals don't have the right to suffer
but this one is noisy and jerky and gave me a traitorous kiss
The real point is that everyone opposes us.

MY SLEEP IS FITFUL AND DISTURBED

The promised land lies along the way
in a place where sleep is fitful
and where there is only a stone for a pillow.

It feels like a beehive.
It is there that God meets us in Person
with a new late-maturing Cauliflower species – "Ultra-Snow Mountain"

We continued promenading there, until near three,
when she said I must lay down by her on her bed, and rest myself,
She was postured in a way that portrayed her
as in both moral and physical decline

she loosened my riding habit, took off my bonnet and said
"You can make a Guinea pig do what ever you want
if you just keep telling him how GORDIOUS he is"

The most common inanities passed between us
mingled with thanks, with inflection like a question
reacting to the powerhouse we call the Sun

by letting him rummage her netting box
indulging in the grossest profanity
and generating a vapour cap above

all was lifted up – the springs of nature rose above their levels
And at the same time some poor wanker necro in half undress
was kissing, fingering and licking Shelene's pussy.

"You have had quite a shock, cousin," she declared
under a superb lustre which shed a quantity of its honours
upon my best merino coat, sprinkling it handsomely with spermaceti.

So far, she have proven to be very cosy,
with an explosion thousands of times stronger than the Hiroshima bomb
(Image of a growing lava dome)

Despite the amount of screen time they shared
it took two decades to convince the terrorists
that they were better off bargaining than fighting

the eight-hour day increasingly a fiction
kneeling by his wife, clasping her to his bosom
as people remained closed inside themselves

It is extremely difficult to achieve perfect randomness
the Sun will not always shine just enough and not too much
But I read, and make such memorandum as I can.

ABOUT THIS BOOK

Every poem in this book is titled with a question from the MMPI, or Minnesota Multiphasic Personality Inventory, a psychological test consisting of 566 true/false questions that has been the benchmark for determining people's mental pathologies as well as their fitness for court trials and military service since the 1930s. Updated in 1989, the MMPI-2 is still relied upon for the same purposes today.

After my interest in the test was piqued by online articles, I found a PDF copy of the original test on a South African web site by searching for strings of phrases from questions published in these same articles.

Once I had access to all the questions, I began to use them to write the poems themselves by feeding phrases from the statements into internet search engines and piecing the poems together from the results pages. This process was a little different for each poem. For instance, for "I LOVED MY FATHER" some results might come from a search for "LOVED MY FATHER" +turtleneck, some from "HATED MY FATHER", some from "HATED MY FATHER" +pussy; etc. I might also then replace words or phrases in the results.

In some cases (mainly in the poems that make use of more archaic language) I followed a link from the search engine page to gather material from an actual web page, but for most poems I did not feel the need to stray from the search results themselves.

The title *The Anger Scale* also comes from online articles about the test. Apparently the MMPI has nine "scales" by which to judge its results, and the "psychopathic deviate" scale, or Scale 4, is sometimes referred to as "the anger scale".

AUTHOR PHOTO BY DREW GARDNER

Katie Degentesh lives in New York City. Her poems and essays have appeared in *Shiny, Fence, New American Writing* and various other periodicals and anthologies. She has an MA in Creative Writing from the University of California, Davis. This is her first book.

COLOPHON

This book is set in the Berthold Baskerville and Interstate
font families. Berthold Baskerville was designed by Günter
Gerhard Lange in 1980, based on the famous type introduced
by British printer John Baskerville between 1752 and 1757,
for the Berthold typefoundry. Interstate, based on the signage
alphabets of the United States of America's Federal Highway
Administration, was designed by Tobias Frere-Jones in 1993
and 1994 and released by The Font Bureau.